Tap into Your Journey

Finding the meaning of your journey, then live it

Matthieu D. Smite

TAP INTO YOUR JOURNEY

Finding the meaning of your journey, then live it

Copyright © 2021 by Matthieu D. Smite

Tap into your Journey

If you would like to use material from the book for short quotations or occasional page copying for personal or group study, this is permitted (other than for review purposes). However, prior written permission must be obtained on request by emailing the author on **msmite@hotmail.co.uk**.

Published by: Authentic Worth
Website: www.authenticworth.com
ISBN Number: 978-1-8384576-4-8

AUTHENTIC
WORTH

Authentic Worth is bringing worth back into you through storytelling and book writing!

Acknowledgements

Bernadette Miamo Irma

I want to thank a very strong woman dear to my heart. Giving her an Oscar for the sacrifice she's taken for her two children would not be enough. The things I've seen her endure for my sister and I will never be forgotten, and the secret prayers she sends up will always be felt and received. Thank you, mum for everything!

Wilson Smite

I want to thank my father as we've managed to turn things around through understanding, the meaningful conversations we've had such as self-belief and ultimately, being grateful to still have a father. Not only that, you've also given me three younger siblings who I love wholeheartedly that has made me more expectant about life and the decisions I make. Thank you for that!

Tap into your Journey

Melodie River Smite

I love the fact that you are built like mum, not to crack under any circumstances. Thank you for my first little niece. Really and truly, Keyanna is the reason my life has changed. I have unconditional love that can't be described for my niece, but as for you, sis, I want you to know that you are the realist for life and the one after.

Chris Ngugi

I want to thank a dear friend of mine who first turned into a brother and following on to a business partner. One of the attributes you added in my life in times past was to grant several books to read when I was at my lowest. I never told you, but it's helped me broaden my mind to grow immensely. We aren't done yet, but thank you brother; I am grateful!

Tap into your Journey

GOD

I would like to thank everyone God has placed in my life that I've crossed paths and had encounters with. Be it family, friends, associates and colleagues because each one of you has been part of the journey and shaped me in one way or the other. My 30-year journey made me aware why certain things had to occur in my life. With that being said, THANK YOU GOD!

"We all start somewhere.

Where we end up,

well, that's our choice."

Anonymous.

Contents Page

Introduction

AUGUST 2011…

I was living in a vicious cycle for seven years. I was 21 when the thought crossed my mind and only God knows why! My belief at the time was *"God placed us in the struggle as a test to not only make it out of the struggle, but to make us stronger."* Funnily enough, I was in my teenage years when I asked my nan what *Dassi* meant (the middle name she gave me.) Her response to that was *"Only God Knows."*

I've been caught up in the hood lifestyle that I didn't intentionally choose and ran with it due to my surroundings and being a product of my environment just like any other young kid. Being in so much trouble between the ages of 14 to 22 made me realise long after how much stress I put my mother through due to my lifestyle.

Tap into your Journey

I had a strong feeling that she knew I was in a gang, but didn't know how to approach the situation, as I come in and go out of the house without discussing how my day went, neither where I've been or the issues I may be facing. In my head, I kept on saying "She'll be alright; she's strong" although she wondered about her son every day. At times, thoughts, questions, and images crossed my mind including the following:

- *"How would my life turn out if my dad was around?"*
- *"Where would I be by now if he was around?"*
- *"Would I be any different to who I am now?"*

The only person I wanted to blame was my dad for not being present to guide me through life. Due to my involvements in the streets, at the age of 17, I learnt about taking responsibility for my actions due to the first and last offences I received where I could've potentially faced a prison sentence for seven years. A good lesson I escaped! So, like most young black boys growing up in a dysfunctional family, I had two options:

Tap into your Journey

1. I either dwell on it, letting it affect me for all my life or;

2. Keep my chin up and take responsibility for my life and make the most out of it.

Today, I am 31 years of age and am yet to reach my ultimate life goal which is to have complete freedom on the journey of a self-employed lifestyle. I'm aware of the journey each level of success brings.

However, this book will tell you what prompted me to start the journey including the cause and effect belief I adopted once my mind shifted through a decision I stood by.

My Why (Purpose)

I have been able to put together what I've been through thus far. My hope for you reading this book is to positively change your perception about life and inspire you to readjust yourself that would benefit your journey in one way or the other through my life's experiences that I share with you today.

Chapter 1

The Path I Led

I recall blurred memories of my dad from the age of four onwards which took place in Martinique where I was born, happily living with both parents, my older sister and my nan. Things seemed normal, until we moved to France. Growing up as a child, my dad was living with us, and at times, he was absent which felt strange. Not once when my dad wasn't around had I mentioned to my mother, "where is daddy?"

As it became a normal lifestyle, seeing my dad come and go was something I got used to. The situation got to a point where my dad wasn't living with us permanently, but would take my sister and I away for the weekend. His physical presence and communication became more and more minimal as the years went on. Living in France, Paris between the ages of 8 to 12 was interesting, good and fun.

Tap into your Journey

Nonetheless, I can say I had a good upbringing regardless, as my mother made sure we took part in sport activities at a young age and making us travel away from home with the local youth club. Dad would be there from time to time to support us in our sport activities which was helpful.

It got to a stage in our lives, aside my father, where my family moved to the United Kingdom in 2002. The decision was taken from my mum for a better life. Only then, the real absence of my father left a hole. Here I am, finding myself in a school where I knew no words of English at the age of 12. I had to adapt and integrate myself pretty fast. It was easier said than done when class mates mocked my English when attempting to communicate.

Being bullied has never been the case in school, but it is inevitable that kids will laugh at strange accents they often don't hear, especially a French one! So, that alone, made me enter an introverted path at a young age.

Tap into your Journey

I unconsciously didn't build or socialise in most institute places because I kept myself from groups. On top of that, my English was a language I had to perfect before I was confident enough to build relationships. Of course, I eventually made friends from school. Some school friends were the ones I'd meet with on the weekends. After a period of time, as we would hang out in the neighbourhood, we started out with mutual friends which led me to join a local gang.

Outside of the gang environment, it was hard to develop a *"social approach personality"* with other individuals because I didn't know how to. I felt my spirit not allowing me to make the first move which resulted in losing potential opportunities in my years growing up. For instance, opportunities such as forming class mates that could've potentially helped me succeed further in my academic years of studying and growing up in college and university.

On the other hand, being in a gang-cultured environment has somewhat shaped my personal identity in becoming a firm and grounded man against the world when life attacked me with adversities. A tough skin had to be built as you would:

1. Get into street fights and;
2. The police brutality I sometimes encountered.

Nonetheless, the lifestyle I led automatically taught me principles which are now embedded within me. I developed and accepted a rule of thumb, morals and a belief to live by, and in particular, loyalty.

Displaying a form of disloyalty is doomed from the environment I was involved in; to handle problems alone in most cases and not to beg or become needy for anything in life. If you want it, you have to work for it, but not by any means necessary to a point where I'd hurt someone. Shocking right?

Tap into your Journey

Although the gang culture teaches you to do the opposite; in this case, it was something which didn't sit right with me, and to be strictly honest, I wasn't taught that being in the street. My experience was just turf wars.

The absence of my father not being present made me seek something I wasn't aware of at the time. Ironically, it wasn't looking up to someone to feel safe or protected but more for guidance. The first guidance I had was someone older than me saying "If you get rid of these drugs for me, you will receive a motorbike at the end of it!" Oddly enough, that was some sort of guidance, or at least perceived at the time. What kid doesn't want a moped in his teenage life? Did that bike ever come my way? Of course not!

My experience of growing up in London where street gangs were known to be predominant in most areas has made me into the individual that was angry, rude, aggressive, and firm whenever I needed to be, and most importantly, taken seriously and those I encountered who didn't know me. In my eyes, this was the perceived understanding of being a man at the time when I was a young boy. Little did I know I was lost and mislead by my surroundings.

Have you ever been directed to God through your hardships? Due to the serious involvement in postcode wars, what became second nature was constantly watching my back, looking at every car that drove past, and circling the estate I lived in including carrying weapons due to the severity of our actions and number of people who hated us.

As a lot was running through my head, I had trouble mentally every time I found myself at home and was always in deep thoughts which kept me up at night and led me to have conversations with myself.

The only way I would escape or seek some sort of stress-relief was *writing about my situation*. I didn't speak to anyone about the burden I was facing. At the time, I lived with my mother and my older sister.

How do you really open up or approach the situation to your own family? The thoughts in my head were clouded with issues that happened. My main concern was not reaching out to my dad due to feeling like a novice.

I felt as if calling my dad to tell him how I felt was perceived as a form of weakness. It may sound easy to do, but it really wasn't. How do you approach a father you barely have a relationship with? I've never opened up to him as a child and was never conditioned to as I didn't feel led to. How can I open up to him at the age of 21?

Writing was my only therapy that made me feel at ease. It gave me peace for a period of time. It was only then that I felt unspeakable joy in conversing with God. That experience made me realise that God dwells within, and ever since then, I continued building a relationship with God.

Tap into your Journey

I strongly believe my dad did what he could, as there were attempts where he'd call me. Even then, I couldn't open up and our conversations were short and wouldn't say much.

When my dad stayed on the phone for more than 10 minutes, the conversations we had were based on my physical health and looking after my mental state which I was very thankful for.

Remember that I often self-reflected; well, I'd soon realise that what my dad would have to do, was to meet my mother and let life take its course the way it intended to. As those thoughts started coming through my mind, I gradually let go of the anger I had towards my dad and the pain carried within.

My definition of a regular life for a young boy was to attend school, college, study, and participate in different forms of activities or hobbies during the week, and go to a friend's house to hang out with them over the weekend.

Tap into your Journey

Although I did enjoy going to school and college, I would always find myself wasting time, which resulted in not achieving the best grades I could've potentially had. This is the point I was making in terms of having sound guidance from a father-figure which would have set healthy boundaries for my life.

I had no boundaries living with my mother which I thought was really cool; doing what I wanted and when I possibly wanted to. My mother did an excellent job in being a provider, protecting us, putting a roof over our heads, clothing us, feeding us and giving us wise advice; nonetheless, there were no strict boundaries.

This often explains the reason why a lot of young boys growing up seek approval beyond what is at home, which in most cases ends up in the wrong places and eventually affects us fitting in and dealing with societal pressure. One of the decisions I thought long enough which I had to make was whether I would go with being a bad boy for the rest of my life or quit and become an integral man.

Tap into your Journey

Eventually, I grew out of it by analysing what was happening in my life and concluded with this: *"My mum did not leave Africa to lead a life of a bad boy and decided to quit!"* I can now say I made one of the best decisions!

It got to a stage in my life at age 22 when I attended church and was invited from a friend. I felt at home and decided to leave the gang lifestyle behind. I also wanted to get back into education which I eventually did at the start. It was exactly what I needed; a positive distraction from the negative outcome I was indulged in.

I enjoyed both church and university where I studied computer science. On the other hand, I felt another kind of heaviness loading on me. Some may say *Welcome to the early adult life*! However, this time, it was a different type of pressure; *"The pressure of managing."* Managing church responsibilities and the workload I had from university.

Tap into your Journey

What I soon learnt from being around spiritual-likeminded individuals was everything we planned to do or were involved in had to include *prayer*.

Prayer became a habit and eventually a lifestyle. The only prayer I grew up knowing before I stepped foot into a church was Matthew 6: 9-15 (The Lord's Prayer), whereas the church I attended on a weekly basis taught me various ways of praying including corporate prayer; the development of a spiritual being having a physical life experience with others.

Unquestionably, prayer was a necessary tool I began enjoying. It came to a point where I took the lead role of conducting prayer meetings. I can still remember the first time I opened a church service with prayer. It was a congregation of just under 200 members. My nerve levels were high! I knew what I had to do; however, I was not fully prepared and didn't know what to say. Once, I took the microphone, stepped in front of the congregation and closed my eyes to pray.

Instantly, I felt the Holy Spirit taking full control over my mouth. All of a sudden, everything flowed out. My close friends can tell you how often I struggled to express myself verbally. How I managed to do this for the first time in front of a crowd was remarkable!

The experience was definitely life changing as it endorsed me to look at myself differently, but furthermore, it made me seek out the spiritual side of life and ask myself questions. I became more conscious of my connection with God on a daily basis which made me worry less about the issues of life and the situations I was going through at the time.

Exercising prayer helps me have a better understanding about life. If I encounter any sort of confusion, I know that God is present to remind me to let go and let Him take its course. It got to the stage where I would have casual conversations with God about everything.

Attending church in my early 20s helped me reinforce and involve God in all that I partake in and not to be unrighteous, remembering how far He brought me from.

Living a care-free life full of happenstance to leading a righteous life filled with peace and joy was all I needed. Just by establishing a real relationship with God has been a real structure in my life which I didn't realise at the time. Perhaps, this was surely the guidance I needed.

Remember when I mentioned that I was in deep thoughts? Well, when I started writing, I found God within me. This is exactly what I mean by having a real relationship with the Father. Start having genuine and honest discussions with yourself and you will eventually encounter the Presence of God.

It is a good feeling to know we have the Holy Spirit looking after us, caring for us, protecting us, and ultimately, providing for us in terms of opportunities, opening the right doors and closing the wrong ones, and hearing Him speak from within to steer us in the right direction. You could be lonely at this moment in time, but John 14:16 says:

"And I will pray to the Father, and He shall give you another Comforter that He may abide with you forever."

God is the Divine One who rules and operates throughout the universe. God created us in His own image, although we have never seen Him physically. The Holy Spirit is within us on a daily basis. In my experience thus far, my journey of spirituality is simply encountering another realm besides what I see with my physical eyes. Question(s):

- Have you ever had a dream and woke up feeling as if it was real?
- Have you ever dreamt of a vision, a goal or a mission and achieved it?

  - This is what I mean by another realm.

Tap into your Journey

- Have you ever had a dream, woke up and came across that same dream with your physical eyes?
- If *yes*, this is the Holy Spirit beyond our imagination and what we know
- If *no*, you are yet to encounter this experience sooner or later!

The church helped me to become more equipped and spiritually ready, preparing for spiritual warfare. Having an enhanced relationship with God has made me aware of the importance to understand and solve my problems from a spiritual perspective in prayer. I did this by working on my personal development which led me to comprehend my emotional and mental health.

Whether you are religious or not, acquiring a level of understanding in your mental, emotional and spiritual well-being will eventually enhance the way you see the world. When this level of understanding reaches a certain height, you will more likely control your environment and what occurs around you.

Tap into your Journey

You will be able to alter your reactions through your mental state and control the feelings in your mind that cause you to make wrong decisions.

If I was to describe prayer in one word, it would be **'extraordinary!'** Eventually, it got to the point where I quit my job I was working for without looking for another role. I was unhappy and decided to leave after giving it a good thought. My mother and a good friend told me this was a bad idea and how I shouldn't have left. I didn't listen, not because of stubbornness but because I believed in myself to obtain a greater opportunity.

I decided to take one week off to rest from working and sought out other roles within the second week. By the third week, I was employed in another organisation.

I managed to find a better opportunity where I was accepted which made me realise, although the chances may not have been in my favour, I made it happen! This little experience gave me greater belief that shaped my world with a positive mindset.

Tap into your Journey

Whether it's declaring positive words of affirmation or good thoughts, the fruits will eventually manifest. One month in the working environment and a flashback came to my mind: *day-dreaming and working in an official corporate office with a suit.*

Amazed at how far I'd come, I had a dream as a child in France that *when I grow up, I want to work in a nice office.*" That was the small vision I had, and now, this has come into existence. I often saw myself and aspired to be that type of individual. Here I am; a Business Development Manager working in Canary Wharf. Of course, it was exciting as prior to that, I'd worked in stadiums, retail, and agencies including sales roles which I am very grateful for.

However, it wasn't about the title or the positions. It was the fact that I made the change to aim higher on my own terms with the belief that it gave me. However, this was God demonstrating to me that anything is possible with Him.

"Life isn't about finding yourself,

it's about creating yourself.

So, live the life you've imagined!"

Henry David Thoreau.

Chapter 2

A Higher Level of Understanding

I made a conscious decision to step away from what was no longer benefitting me, due to the misalignment, disbelief and other aspects that didn't fit with my purpose. It took nearly a year to take time out of my church.

In my opinion, churches don't have an immediate responsibility to make one discover their identity. I believe churches are put in place to contribute in helping individuals unite together.

Leaving wasn't easy as the relationships and responsibilities built over the years grew, but a decision had to be made in order to seek a higher level of understanding. After four years of attending the same church throughout, I felt I was being kept under the same cloud. Though a cloud can be bright, it often can get blurry and foggy, although I definitely gained confidence under that cloud.

However, as seasons changed and evolved, certain things prone to me no longer served me as an individual. Prior to my departure, I started receiving a few questions including the following:

- What practice did we have before religion?

- Why have I been hearing a repetitive messaged being preached?

- Why is the preaching based on a particular aspect of Christianity?

- Why don't the churches speak on different topics?

- Why don't they teach on how to become responsible men and follow purpose before influencing marriage at a young age?

... and many other questions.

Tap into your Journey

This felt like culture, rather than having a deeper personal relationship with God. I understood that due to the upbringing and mindsets of members in the church, I assumed that they had one way of thinking; however, for me, I wanted more of a stronger connection with God above anything else.

Those questions couldn't be answered, let alone asked in the church because, to me, it would be seen as deviating the church's purpose. As I endeavored to get my questions answered, I managed to get a few responses. The answers gave me clarity with confidence over confusion.

It wasn't that I started questioning God, but I started questioning the organisation of the church; in other words, the people, because we are the church. The clarity I received, to me, gave me further understanding. Some of the sermons were no longer benefitting me, rather, it was for the people's own interests.

Tap into your Journey

I remembered a few years ago why I started attending church and was solely due to:

1) Comfortability and;
2) Being a better individual.

In every service, I would take what was applicable to me and apply them in my life to become better, as well as being responsible with my duties in the church. Along the years, as I became more intrigued, I wanted to find the truth to what we hear from time to time; what *'religion'* is.

Part of this made me reject the term *religion* and enabled me to become more aware of a higher form of understanding. This understanding made me conscious of the flashbacks I was going through several years ago, that led me in entertaining a low-level mindset. Take a look:

- **2004 to 2012** – This included several incidents due to gang affiliations.

Tap into your Journey

2013 – This included my attempt to leave the street life, stay home, study and attend church.

2014 – This included applying for several jobs, being unqualified and rejected by all.

2015 – This included withdrawing from university for failing a module exam three times.

2016 – This included getting fired from a job on the second day after my birthday.

2017 – I was stabbed.

Although we have 365 days in a year, my experiences caused a negative impact throughout each year. This influenced my mental state and made it difficult and challenging throughout my 20s. The higher understanding that came to me was *you reap what you sow* (Galatians 6:7). I'd have to eventually face the consequences of my actions.

Tap into your Journey

A very simple saying to comprehend and a statement we often hear multiple times, but difficult to apply it. Once I removed myself from the negative mindset I was entertaining between the ages of 14 to 22, I took upon myself the responsibility to redefine and adjust myself. It took up until the age of 26 to see my mindset shift positively. All the wrong moves I made in the past taught me great lessons that I am still learning up till now and is what makes me who I am today.

I was 27 when I got stabbed, although it wasn't due to anything personal or gang-related. It was because I defended my friend when a fight occurred whilst trying to protect him. At the time, retaliation crossed my mind.

It could've been very easy for me to pick up a weapon and retaliate, but it wasn't worth it, due to what I knew then. In the situation I was in, it would be easy to assume that retaliation is what makes us superior, respected and being feared in most cases. Really and truly, not having to retaliate shows and proves great strength by controlling your emotions and letting go.

Tap into your Journey

In 2011, Floyd Mayweather fought for his WBC title boxing fight against his opponent Victor Ortiz. The fight only lasted for four rounds, but if you watch each round carefully, you'd come to an agreement that Victor Ortiz's punches weren't landing on his opponent Floyd Mayweather as much as he wanted to.

On the other hand, Floyd Mayweather was winning points after points. On the fourth round, things were getting intense as Floyd was giving combos after combos. As they held onto each other in the moment, Victor Ortiz used his head to gently hit Mayweather's head. The referee gave Ortiz a light warning and the fight rapidly took off again.

Suddenly, after a few seconds, Ortiz started to get clean shots he wanted to land all along, but in the midst of it all, he launched his body to hit Mayweather with his head, and eventually, Mayweather happened to suffer a bruise on his lips, as Ortiz let his emotions get the best of him to the point where he lost control.

Tap into your Journey

The referee stopped the fight and took a point away from Ortiz. Mayweather seemed shocked, but kept his cool and had his head in the fight. By the time the referee had given the go-ahead for the fight to continue, Ortiz was still proclaiming his forgiveness towards Mayweather for his wrong move.

Mayweather landed two clean punches that led him to win the fight by KO. Some may say it was sucker punch by Floyd, but one thing for sure, the one fighter kept his emotions under control whilst the other fighter did not. What do you think could have happened if Floyd Mayweather headbutted Victor Ortiz as it happened to him twice and lost his emotions? Consider the following:

1. A point lost to Mayweather
2. This would have potentially resulted in an expensive fight cancelled if both rivals lost their cool instead of following the boxing rules.

Tap into your Journey

Another example I want to use is the death of a young American music artist by the name of *King Von* who was shot and killed in 2020. His involvement of a street fight cost him his life with a rival gang he had issues with. I've never heard of King Von prior to him being tragically killed, but from his death, his name rang intentionally in my mind, which made me curious to find out whom and what King Von was about.

From the research I gathered, he was deep in the streets with allegedly murderous charges he once faced. Although he was not found guilty for the charges against him, it was clear that the ongoing battle in Chicago costed many young lives before King Von's passing.

King Von's poor decision of not being able to leave the nonsense behind him, whilst doing very well for himself financially as well as his music career, and looking after his loved ones costed him his life.

Tap into your Journey

We all have childhood friends that we intend to bring with us when we make it to the top, especially those that have helped us in our pasts. However, the TRAP occurs when one fails to recognise that coming from a place of violence costs many souls to lose their lives in the streets, and sadly, King Von happened to be one of them.

When I was 27 up until the age of 31, I reached the upmost peaceful state in life. Between those four years, I've been able to gracefully enjoy and reap from the wise decisions made, setting my goals and achieving them.

To me, this has become my new reward and I stand on what goes around will eventually come back around. If you've been rewarded negatively whilst doing good to others, be patient; your time will eventually come when you least expect it.

Tap into your Journey

Nature reveals that there is always a cause to an effect. A tree can only grow with the seed planted. A tree can't flourish without rain, and over a period of time, our bodies are less likely to function without nutrients and water.

Our bodies are less likely to function best without rest and sleep. If I was to approach a wild animal in peace and wanting to take their offspring for my own good, the entire herd will charge at me and attack.

On the other hand, one could make a certain amount of money and use it to sell drugs, however, the effects of those actions will be based on law enforcements that will eventually result in prison. Be wise enough to see, acknowledge, and adjust yourself to live an abundant life.

Everything has been created for our benefit and success. How do I know that? Let's look at the following:

Tap into your Journey

1) Look around you; everything was created by a thought which initially became a result *(in reference to Genesis 1)*

2) After being rejected by 20 plus agencies, I decided to create an agency with my good friend.

Redefine your mindset by reassessing your position in life and adjust yourself in order to tap into the higher level of understanding.

"Life is too short and too precious to spend it with many distractions accumulating perishable treasures. Let's try rather, to understand life's true meaning to enrich our souls."

Socrates.

Chapter 3

Thyself

Life can be a puzzle; you won't always know which pieces fit until you take the time to figure it out. I was on a journey which enabled me to discover myself through life's experiences. These inevitable experiences we go through helps us know ourselves little by little. It's unfortunate that some people don't take the time to know and understand who they are due to their environments and lifestyles they choose to keep.

For those who manage to stay clear from environments that prevent them from moving forwards, will eventually tap into their greatest strength and start to understand why certain situations had to happen the way they did. Valuable life lessons, either negative or positive will help you understand life from a bigger perspective and put the puzzle pieces together. Life teaches us the following:

Tap into your Journey

1. *Making sense of what you had to go through*
2. *Making sense of why you are here on earth*
3. *Making sense of a life filled with purpose*

From time to time, you will encounter various trials which will cause you to grow stronger and eventually, shape your life. This includes the people that are attached to you and will either have a positive or negative impact, as well as the environment you grew up in.

We may have several questions about life, however at times, those questions may not always have the applicable answers. Nonetheless, through relentless pursual of questions unanswered, this will make you seek out the unknown.

Life is unknown because we don't know how tomorrow will look like, however, it will make you search within yourself. In other words, an intuition will speak to you.

God Himself is the One that grants us the freedom to know who we are and the gifts we have within us. Some value it and others don't. It is important to help you understand what is guiding you along the way.

In terms of my own journey and how I managed to understand who I was came at a time where I intentionally segregated myself from most people and started enjoying my own company for a season. When this happened, I looked at everything from an external point of view which helped me to identify situations that wouldn't have been understood from an internal perspective.

"I'll use a boxing fight as an example – there is a reason why a referee is in the ring and three to five extra side-line referees are outside of the ring. Although they play different roles, what the referee sees from an external perspective is usually different from looking in the ring."

Tap into your Journey

Therefore, by stepping outside of the box, it gave me more time to spend with myself and my own thoughts, which led me to pay attention to my 30 years' life experiences. Those experiences enabled me to tap into my intuition. Bear in mind that *being alone* and *loneliness* are not the same.

My aim is not to make you feel lonely and segregate yourself from your connections. As human beings, we all need connections, but making a decision to go through a state of solitude for a period of time is healthy and does not reflect on abandoning your loved ones and those that are surrounded by you.

A study gathers that the more disconnected you are with others, the more pain you will feel internally, which is equivalent to emotional dysfunction. A form of human connections helps in several ways as it often speaks volumes in our lives and helps us become better individuals. If we are always left to our own devices, we will always see life from our own perspective and not learn from others.

Tap into your Journey

This is a crucial part to our individual journey. Without it, we may go into survival mode and become complacent. In my case at the time, this wasn't what I needed. One of the ways I notice people who speak into my life is by reading books during a solitude period. Although I didn't fully disconnect myself from my friends, I made sure that I kept a healthy distance to decline any forms of social activities.

In a broken home where a father is absent and placed in an environment where there is idolatry, I was a product of my environment; joining the street life nine times out of ten. I simply wanted more for myself. It was through my solitude that my intuition led me to ask, seek and knock.

Some things I had asked, sought for and knocked were answered, and gave me more clarity about myself on how to attain and manifest the things I was after as young teenager. **Let me break down the definition of the three words below:**

Tap into your Journey

ASK: There are two kinds of asking:

1) Physically
2) Spiritually

We know the physical term of asking. Before you ask verbally, you would have thought about it first. I retained that thought in my mind weekly, monthly, even yearly, because it had to be what I was after.

Retaining the thought continuously became a routine where I started asking from a spiritual perspective. I thought about it long enough to the point that it inevitably made me seek a higher calling which led me onto the next stage. *Seek:*

SEEK: I never knew the true meaning of this word that meant: "attempt to find." I knew when to use the word but never knew the exact definition. That's the French in me! Yes, up to this day, I can still be like that, however, the only way of attempting to find it was through taking action. I had to plan and understand how to go about what I desired. **We do this when seeking for a job opportunity**.

Which direction should I be taking? I never knew how I'd get there which was often frustrating. At the time, I'd only plan it in my thoughts and tell myself what I ought to do, until I realised that writing it down on paper compelled me to take more action. The seeking eventually compelled me to the next stage. *Knocking:*

KNOCKING: The spiritual aspect of knocking never made sense to me at the time. As I already knew what knocking meant, I defined it as: 'keep on asking until a door of opportunity opens.' All of this only made sense to me once I arrived at one of my goals' destination.

To define knocking in a form of achieving what you want out of life, you have to be *consistent*. Let me give you an example of what I went through. There was a time I was working with a good friend, Noël for his removal company in the city, Cannon Street doing an office move.

Tap into your Journey

At the time, Mak and Sons removal was helping me get by as I didn't have a job, but in my mind, I always wanted to work in the city wearing a suit and feeling good about myself. Not only to have an image, but wanting more for myself.

As we took part in the removal job, I wasn't totally focused as I kept admiring by-standers walking pass the van. You can imagine them looking well-presented in their suits, and using their phones to discuss business. Noël noticed that I wasn't focused and asked me: "Look at you! You want to be just like them, don't you?"

I smiled and kept quiet, as he knew I aspired to be like that. A few months later, I became one of those men in a suit working in Cannon Street for an international events company.

In order for me to knock, I envisioned myself in their shoes and being in their position from the start. I kept picturing myself in a smart suit, and conducted myself like one of them.

Tap into your Journey

Some of my friends noticed a change in me to the point that one of them referred to me as having a *conservative character*. That is the spiritual aspect of knocking as well as applying the other two components: *asking* and *seeking*.

The most amazing revelation to all of this is the discovery of what prayer really is:

- To become!
- Our God-given power is to BECOME;
- To become what we envision.

Have you ever done something you were proud of? Have you ever accomplished a goal you wanted to reach? How did you feel once you achieved it? Good right? But, most likely powerful too. We often feel it and proclaim proudly how powerful we have come, but hardly see beyond it. This is exactly what God wants for us because He dwells within YOU.

"You don't look out there in the sky for God, you look within you."

Alan Watts.

Chapter 4

Relationship Outlook

There are several types of relationships between friends and those we classify as potential intimate partners. Some people may claim that they are *self-made*; however, I want you to ask yourself this question…is it really possible that one will make it to the top successfully without the help of others? I strongly disagree! Though relationships are important towards our progress, relationships will either make or break us. Let's go in deeper:

Friends

From school days to our adult lives, we interact with many individuals whom we've become friends with. Along the course of the journey, we formed and continue to form great relationships with those that remain by our side. I've had several types of friends in the course of my journey.

Tap into your Journey

Through having those friends, I've understood that not every one of them can fulfil all aspects that a friend can offer. In other words, it's not all areas that I can fulfil in my friends' lives either. Each one plays different roles within a friendship which is necessary to identify at the early stages. Why do we have friends? We have friends for the following reasons:

- A time of fun and to create great memories
- A time to potentially waste
- A time of trust (to confide in)
- A time of support (financially, mentally, emotionally) one way or another
- A time of prayer
- A time to stick behind/beside you through storms
- A time to push, elevate or help you recognise your worth
- A time to work and build something substantial (in rare cases.)

Tap into your Journey

I may have missed out on other areas that friends may serve in our lives, but it's for you to identify which category your friends fall into and accept the role each one plays.

Once you've done that, it also becomes easier to accept the role each one can't play in order to have peace of mind and prevent yourself from being affected by the frustration's life can bring from time to time with friendships.

Depending on the nature of siblings, however, it may be challenging to build relationships with them as we're always around them 24/7. Sometimes, we do need healthy boundaries to maintain the flow of family bonding.

Nonetheless, we tend to create strong bonds with our friends that we are comfortable calling them bro or sis, to the point where we proudly proclaim that *they are our sisters and brothers from another mother*.

Notwithstanding, even those close friends can often become difficult to comprehend, hence the reason why it is healthy to have more than *one* friend. When you fail to comprehend one friend, other people around you can make you understand what it is you've failed to realise.

Intimate Relationships

If I had to change anything about my previous relationship, I wouldn't change anything. For the simple fact that I learnt valuable aspects of myself which prepared me for the next. I know where I could've pushed myself and done a better job as a partner and a man.

I also know how I'd handle not only situations more efficiently, but conduct myself more competently. Not to say I didn't play my part in the relationship I was in; I played my position to what I believed it to be good enough.

Tap into your Journey

We will always have our own perspectives on how an ideal situation should be until it is shaken by reality. Nonetheless, I didn't break boundaries or trust, but I eventually found out, besides these qualities, there was more that were needed to maintain a good relationship as a whole.

However, my position wasn't executed well enough to the point where it could keep the satisfaction flowing. It is one thing to gain whatever we are after, but completely another aspect to maintain whatever it may be that we've gained during the relationship.

These are some of the challenges I faced at the time which I want to share with you:

- Lack of leadership in certain situations
- Lack of mental and sexual stimulation
- Lack of career progression
- Lack of financial progression

Tap into your Journey

How else would I have known where my defaults were and what I'd had to adjust to, if I didn't go through what I did in the relationship? When you are in your first relationship, especially at a young age, more often, it doesn't necessarily consist of a solid foundation, although you believe to build it to the best of your ability and eventually make it a long-lasting partnership with your significant.

A break up is usually what makes individuals stronger and causes them to be aware of their foundation that ought to be built independently first, however, this depends on the person's mindset.

I didn't beat up myself for the weaknesses I had at the time. I looked at it as lessons and learning curves to empower my ability to flourish. Only when it ended, I looked at that journey as a ranking pyramid.

Imagine this: at the top, you have everything you wanted in a relationship and acquiring the things you lacked to be at the bottom and let that be your starting point. Just as stepping into your first relationship, it will always be your starting point. Within that starting point, you will grow as time goes on to realise the abilities you possess and the abilities you lack. Remember, no one is perfect.

How else will you reach and acquire all the skills and abilities that is needed in a relationship if you've never experienced being in one or guided by somebody who has walked on that path?

If you expected to have each quality or aspect mentioned above from your teenage years up into your late 20s, I am here to remind you that not even Romeo could get a woman he first loved which was Rosaline to love him back.

Romeo eventually moved on to another woman called Juliet and fell in love at first sight when he saw her at a party (*Romeo was definitely tripping!*) even after getting Juliet, they didn't last due to unforeseen circumstances.

Tap into your Journey

Tell yourself: *"It's just part of life; everything I go through was meant to empower me!"* Be empowered and become better by acquiring the added qualities that life teaches you.

Being the only man living in a household with two females (my mother and sister) one of the key lessons my mother passed onto me is how to treat women due to how she raised my sister and I.

On the contrary, the other things she couldn't teach me was the essence of loyalty, being a protector and how to lead our own lives, but I knew where I got those principles from – THE STREETS! Even though we may not have the right person to guide us through our journey, eventually, life will take us to our individual destinies.

"Better to do something imperfectly than to do nothing flawlessly!"

Robert Schuller.

Chapter 5

Broken Attachment

Anything you can't stop dwelling on can become an idol which you get attached to, both emotionally and mentally; you continuously want more. We feel that our attachments bring happiness due to the state of pleasure it gives. The attachment I experienced was of being in a relationship, which at the time, I didn't realise my eagerness for it, until the relationship wasn't fruitful and ended.

The love I once exchanged had a positive feeling whilst being in the relationship, despite the fluctuations from time to time. However, I realised the negative effects it had on me when my relationship faltered over a period of time. I didn't comprehend as to why this had such a negative impact until a thought process emerged which made me realise that I was still too invested in the relationship.

Tap into your Journey

It started to make sense of the negative side effects I was going through which included being unproductive at work, isolating myself from everyone and being antisocial.

However, becoming accustomed to a positive feeling that gives you emotional satisfaction, relative to knowing that it will no longer be there was definitely a lesson learnt and I had to live without it. Once, I was made aware of what attachment felt like. I was able to effectively work on myself and discipline the negative feelings, as this was the only way forward.

It can be easy to rush into another relationship to soothe the pain, but this was not the answer. My priority was a matter I took on myself. As painful as it was, without the experience, I wouldn't have thought to put myself first. I simply recommend that you don't forget yourself when it comes to being in a relationship; you are just as important as the other individual.

Tap into your Journey

Putting yourself last can result in sacrificing your priorities to meet the needs of the other individual. In essence, the healing process happened when I kept myself occupied with what was more important, including my *purpose*.

It may be easier said than done, but it's best to learn from the pain that separation brings and eventually, work on the internal pain and heal. We have seen materialistic possessions come and go. As perishable items never last, what is the purpose of getting attached to them?

I continue learning how to discipline my mindset to not become emotionally attached to possessions and people. It's about having a balanced perspective on both. *Time* and *focus* were the two contributing factors that helped me in the process of being set free from the emotional attachment. The replacement of this attachment was to dedicate more time on improving my physical health.

Tap into your Journey

I felt I was mentally stable to deal with the situation, despite the grief. The constant focus became about how I could improve my wellbeing and felt a different sense of satisfaction. Taking care of my emotions made me enter a space of self-love I never knew.

The most important factor is not to lose the primary focuses; your mental and emotional health. In most cases, when we look good, we feel good, and if we nurture our minds with positivity, we produce productivity.

When our finances are healthy, we eventually see positive changes which impacts our loved ones and give freely. Ultimately, it equates to self-love and the replacement of broken attachments, although these lessons we can't always avoid, but we can choose to learn from them and move on.

"You only lose what

you cling to."

Buddah.

Chapter 6

Finding Your Feet Again

As a child, I had many ideas of what I wanted to become; a fireman, a footballer and other aspirational desires. As a kid watching TV in my mother's house, it was the norm. When movies were being played, I'd recall men working in prestige office buildings in white t-shirts and ties in front of their computers. I got attracted to the smartly dressed conduct and positioned myself as if it were me.

As the years caught up with me from starting primary school, to secondary school, going to college and attending university, circumstances got in the way and became a distraction which blurred the vision I had for my life. The image I had wasn't stored at the forefront of my mind due to what I encountered at the time. Fast forward to the early 20s where those years tested and challenged me.

Tap into your Journey

I felt lost due to my antics, however, I eventually found my feet in my mid 20s where I realised that what I wanted to become and the career path I was working to embark on, was the envisioned end goal.

How I managed to find my feet again

I simply segregated myself from the environment I was in at the time, whilst enjoying my own company. After years of being distracted by my surroundings, there were periods in my life where I made the decision to stay out of trouble by spending time at home looking for a job. It was tough staying put and spending time building my future.

I received a phone call one early morning from my dad. The only thing I remember him telling me was this: *"Think of your niece; think of your little brother and your sisters. If you end up going to prison, you will be the most selfish person."*

I never thought of what my dad said and how it could've affected my siblings if I landed myself in prison. That conversation left me contemplating and led me to make firm decisions to quit and make my life count. When I took a break from the job search, I would watch TV and at times, pick up my Bible and read a few passages to keep me going for encouragement.

Eventually, after days and weeks of not getting anywhere with the job search, I watched an American TV program called *The Million Dollar Listing*; American real estate tycoons selling properties worth millions and brokers that were getting no less than five figures as their commission.

At that moment, I had a flashback of the vision I once had as a kid. It was at this moment I told myself **"YES! THIS IS WHAT I WANT TO DO!"** I started investing more in the program, the luxury houses, the mansions and the apartments they were selling.

My focus came back to me; I wasn't applying for random vacancies as my aim was to get through the door of an estate agent. I started looking for anything to do with *lettings*.

Tap into your Journey

I came across a lettings negotiator training course, although I had no experience and decided to enrol. The course taught the key skills on how to become a practical lettings negotiator.

I had to take exams for the Level 2 Award in Residential Property Management Practice. I learnt not only how to make cold calls, but enhancing my pitch on what to say to landlords, offer marketing services to landlord's properties and generate reliable ideal tenants, conducting viewings and negotiating deals to rent houses and flats.

Although I was only getting paid commission, I decided to apply for several estate agency roles once the course ended. I took a leap of faith and handed out CV's to several independent agencies and the main corporative agencies. This included applying online to signing up with jobsite agencies and sending direct emails to several companies which was a lot of work.

Tap into your Journey

At the time, I was granted an interview with a small agency, although it did not proceed further, and eventually I started to become unmotivated to continue.

After many attempts, I managed to ace an interview from an independent estate agency and was offered a role to start on my birthday! I was excited and couldn't wait to start. The day finally came; I was eager to learn on the job, pick up the phone and make calls, wanting to perform better than the existing staff members.

I managed to get two viewings on the same day and I conducted both, and had to report how it went towards the end of the day. That was my first day at work completed. At one point, I remember meeting with the woman I was dating at the time after work. Everything felt easy and sooth.

Day two at work; we go again! I was anticipating to use the phone and handle business. The manager called me into the office and handed me an envelope. The manager's words were: "*I have to let you go, but this is your pay for the hours you did yesterday.*" I was speechless and didn't know what to say. After a few seconds of realising what the manager said, I managed to ask why? The manager responded saying *"I don't believe you are qualified enough."*

How does a company offer a job to an individual after having the interview and a day's trial to then decide the individual isn't qualified enough?? I took a deep breath and walked off. The envelop has the cheque of a day's work; £75.00.

Everything seemed great but I was wrong. I gave up applying for the role and was no longer in my interest to work as an estate agent. Telling my mum and girlfriend at the time was painful.

As a man, some may feel like they have failed and I felt exactly that. Things were becoming worse as money was low. Every other day I thought of going back to the street and hustle. *"A man's got to do what a man's got to do!"* was at the forefront of my mind. However, I made a promise that I would not go back on the streets.

Tap into your Journey

Throughout the rough journey, I happened to reconnect with a good friend that was from the same neighbourhood. He managed to be doing well and became one of the top salesmen in his job.

We spent time with each other quite a lot, but despite him being one of the top sales representatives at his place of work, he, like everyone else, was going through difficulties. I managed to help and remove one of the burdens he was going through. He was thankful and returned the favour by offering me a job at the place he once worked.

From being around each other on a daily basis, we spoke of my experience of trying to become an estate agent and partaking in the training course I did at the time. This conversation sparked the both of us and agreed to eventually start our own business within the property industry. His exact words were *"ARE YOU ON IT?"* and my response was *"ARE YOU ON IT?"*

We both had a vision which gave us *purpose*. We eventually made the vision come to reality and we are now proudly running our own property management service business. What would've happened if I decided to go back on the streets for being impatient due to lack of money? Sometimes, I ask myself that, and only God knows the answer to that question.

There will be times in your life where it will feel as if you are losing, but eventually, you will win. Being lost in life (or on your journey) contains real blessings in disguise. You could be unknowingly gifted and spiritually unaware of your inner voice; however, you eventually decide to tap into it and realise it was already in you.

What I went through enabled me to understand that it guided me in making the right decisions, giving me the answer to step out of what was my vulnerable situation. As I readjusted, I put myself in a position to follow my purpose by surrounding myself with the right people. Everything will happen as it's ordained to be, as long as you can make the right adjustments and stick to it.

Tap into your Journey

Who and what played a great part in my life?

Knowing my friend from the past built our trust between each other as we reconnected. The bond we built stemmed from recognising that he always wanted more out of his situation besides accumulating money for the sake of it. When my friend managed to help me be a part of the company he once worked at, I saw the other side of Chris being on top of his game amongst his peers.

Proverbs 13:20 (NIV) says:

"Walk with the wise and become wise, for a companion of fools suffers harm."

It didn't take me long to thrive within the same department which I managed to not only do well in, but work my way up in achieving two different positions. The ability to show and prove my worth was what I believed to have embedded in me. The qualities I possessed that enabled me to demonstrate my effectiveness in the organisation was what awakened my belief to harness my abilities and work on my own personal vision.

Being in different institutions made me realise what I was after; the level of freedom I wanted to reach. I remember being in school, determined to make it in life including completing a PhD.

Going through all those academic stages to have the life I wanted seemed attainable on one hand, and daunting on the other. After failing in my academic years, I realised that I had to commit to my craft, be consistent and have determination which will take me higher.

The responsibility I've taken thus far has given me a taste of freedom and it's being able to work towards complete freedom. Along the journey, the motivation it has given me to move forwards and reach my full potential was certain to happen. This is what I want for you too! Whether you are academically smart or not.

Tap into your Journey

Taking full responsibility for my life helped me not to fall into the entitlement trap of assuming I deserved everything, but rather, to love my family and friends to make them proud.

Former President; Barack Obama's favourite line phrase was this: *"I am responsible and take full responsibility."* Accountability is a key trait a president must have if he or she ought to run for their own country.

Focus on you! You are running your own life by taking responsibility for your actions, no matter what situation you are in. You ought to take control of the outcome and change the circumstances you end up in.

"Not until we are lost,
do we begin to understand
ourselves."

Henry David Thoreau.

Chapter 7

The Ultimate Prize

The questions I'd ask myself regarding the years of my life's experiences is, what is the ultimate prize in this world? The answer is: *LOVE*:

"For God so loved the world that He gave His one and only Son, that whoever believes in Him shall not perish but have eternal life." – John 3:16 (NIV)

The entire scripture is important, but I would like to emphasize on, "For GOD so loved the world that He gave." Throughout my life's experiences, it made me realise that whatever you give out, it will eventually return back to you.

Although there are many lessons to learn ahead, my 31 years on earth has taught me and is continuing to teach many key lessons. If you've ever wondered or asked why a certain individual is so blessed, analyse the way they conduct and handle themselves, their work ethic and determination invested into their passions. I've learnt to witness that the service you give out in good will, shall come back to you from people who will return genuine love. If you were to provide a service with little interest, the love put into that service will reap a small amount back.

A famous quote by **Ray Bradbury** that is often heard of is: *"Love what you do and do what you love."* The effort you put in is a direct reflection of your interests. With that being said, think of exchanging whatever it is you give out of love. The effort you give is a reflection of high interest which equates to the ultimate prize.

This prize comes in different ways to bless you in disguise. It comes in both physical and spiritual forms. The feelings from what you receive after giving is the greatest prize of all; I call it a *soul-filling satisfaction.*

Tap into your Journey

I am going to share what I believe has been my two secrets that haven't been disclosed, so, you are the first to know. These secrets are what I've lived by and seen various manifestations from:

Matthew 6:1, 3-4 (NIV):

"Be careful not to practise your righteousness in front of others to be seen by them. If you do, you will have no reward from your Father in Heaven (3) But when you give to the needy, do not let your left hand know what your right hand is doing (4) so that your giving may be in secret. Then your Father, who sees what is done in secret, will reward you."

The first verse teaches us to have good intentions in helping the less fortunate without drawing attention or publicity to ourselves, but to give without anyone knowing. Every time I find myself helping those in any kind of need, I made sure it stayed between them and my Father in Heaven.

Tap into your Journey

With pure intentions, I've tapped into believing the rewards that have come in my life due to this principle.

Matthew 5:44 (NIV):

"But I tell you, love your enemies and pray for those who persecute you, that you may be children of your Father in Heaven."

The second verse amazes me! Although I was involved in gang rivalries in the past, one practice I often did was citing *"I pray for my enemies"* along with my personal prayers. It wasn't easy praying for them due to the lack of love I had in my heart.

However, it was never a form of hatred. It felt more as if it was a tit for tat and an eye for an eye thing. When I found myself citing this prayer, I was saying it without true meaning, however, once I read it from the Bible and acted on it, that was when it became easier to apply.

Tap into your Journey

Fast forward: when I had major problems with my adversaries who happened to be in the same premises, we shared a few words and decided to part our differences aside and shook hands. They came to an understanding before considering to make peace with me. However, I didn't make the first step; they did.

Once I read the Bible passages, it continued staying with me and gave the added principles to live by. The picture I am portraying is that we will surely reap what we sow, and everything we do in life has to be done with good intentions for one to receive a return of a peaceful life leading to the ultimate prize.

I am grateful that my relationship with my Dad is going great, although we live thousands of miles away from each other. I look at some of my friends who've lost their parents, and it makes me grateful, despite the small differences I once had with my father. I came to a mature understanding with myself to let go of the pain I once felt of an absent father not being present in order to establish a father-son relationship, no matter the distance. Had I held onto the grudges and neglected my father due to what he didn't offer me as a child, it wouldn't have been the answer. I can proudly say that I feel the love through the communication we have and the words spoken.

Although I am on a path to reach my latter goal, my intuition has helped to evaluate my life, and react based on current situations to progress in the upcoming years.

Tomorrow isn't promised and we shouldn't be negligent on the present moment, but to be realistic. Have a clear vision including an action plan that will steer you into the right direction. Whether it's a mental mind space, I always reassess my thoughts from time to time to be the change in my environment, working to the best of my ability, fulfilling my needs and exceed my expectations set.

Examples

Thoughts: If I had negative or toxic thoughts based on a bad situation, I assess them and tell myself I shouldn't let those thoughts turn to reactions that could jeopardise the situation. Therefore, when I find myself angry, I release the anger by trying to remain calm.

Places: These are the locations I've been, lived and worked for in several seasons of my life. I've managed to work in four different industries, as well as encountering, interacting and understanding the differences in people.

Besides Martinique where I was born and living in France from a young age, I've managed to travel to a few countries alone without friends and the experiences taught me several added values.

Material Objects: When you are determined to achieve a specific goal, your mind is likely to dwell on it and think of an action plan. Our job is to mentally entertain and grasp what we desire which will lead us forward in taking action as mentioned in chapter 4. Envisioning is the contributing factor that you should obtain in order for your heart's desires to come to fruition.

Tap into your Journey

Having read The Path I Led, I am believing that it has brought a lot of inspiration, tenacity and determination. My life is a testimony, and through tapping into it, I wasn't aware of the great meaning life had. I believe your journey in life will fall into fruition as you take what comes your way and to embrace every lesson.

"The most important thing is to try and inspire people, so that they can be great in whatever they want to do."

Kobe Bryant.

Tap into your Journey

SELF-EVALUATION

YES ← **Do you currently feel lost or trapped?** → **NO**

I'm glad that you've acknowledged it. Have you ever envisioned the life you desire to live?

← **YES** **Do you feel you're influenced to lead a life you're not in control of?**

← **NO**

YES

NO

Do you have distractions that prevent you from pursuing your dreams?

Are you content with where you are at this stage of your life?

YES

YES

Take the time to segregate yourself. Companionship is good, but life in society often pushes us to put on a front and avoid areas of confrontation, alongside being preoccupied and distracted.

GREAT! Wishing you all the best moving forward in your journey!

By doing so, you will tap into being more aware and responsible with your decision-making and taking steps to progress.

Pay attention for any gradual manifestations. Once you see the realisation of it, don't look back.

Self-development books are great tools to help you take action once you've spent time working on yourself.

By the time you reassess your life's journey, it will shift, attracting the right opportunities and people to you.

References

Dr Philip Weller, (1941), Shakespeare Navigators, Accessed on 15 December 2020, Available at: <https://shakespeare-navigators.com/romeo/Rosaline.html>

Fred Thomas, *King Von*, All Music, Accessed on 20 December 2020, Available at: <https://www.allmusic.com/artist/king-von-mn0003831585/biography?cmpredirect>

Golden Boy Boxing, (2015), Golden Boy Flashback: Floyd Mayweather vs Victor Ortiz, Available at: <https://www.youtube.com/watch?v=vz0p5YqhMrE> Accessed date: 05 June 2019.

Jeff Simon, (2014), The Washington Post, Accessed on 23 June 2019. Available at: <https://www.washingtonpost.com/news/the-fix/wp/2014/07/10/five-bad-things-that-obama-has-said-hes-responsible-for-video/>

Tap into your Journey

Maria Popova, (2012), Brain Pickings, Accessed on 21 December 2020. Available at: <https://www.brainpickings.org/2012/03/09/ray-bradbury-on-doing-what-you-love/>

Noor Lobad, (2020), *Who is King Von? Everything To Know About The Lil Durk And OTF Affiliate,* Hot New Hip Hop, Accessed on 20 December 2020, Available at: <https://www.hotnewhiphop.com/who-is-king-von-everything-to-know-about-the-lil-durk-affiliate-rapper-news.118424.html >

<u>NOTES</u>

<u>NOTES</u>

<u>NOTES</u>

<u>NOTES</u>

_____

_____

_____

_____

_____

_____

_____

_____

_____

_____

_____

_____

_____

_____

_____

_____

_____

_____

_____

NOTES

<u>NOTES</u>

_____

_____

_____

_____

_____

_____

_____

_____

_____

_____

_____

_____

_____

_____

_____

_____

_____

_____

NOTES

<u>NOTES</u>

<u>NOTES</u>

<u>NOTES</u>

Printed in Great Britain
by Amazon